modern
Cocktails
& Appetizers

modern
Cocktails
& Appetizers

Martha Gill

Photographs—Jeff Von Hoene
Cocktail Cuisine—Alix Kenagy
Text—Matthew De Galan

LONGSTREET
Atlanta, Georgia

Published by LONGSTREET PRESS, INC.

A subsidiary of Cox Newspapers, a subsidiary of Cox Enterprises, Inc.

2140 Newmarket Parkway, Suite 122, Marietta, GA 30067

Printed in Hong Kong by Paramount Printing

2nd printing 1998

Library of Congress Catalog Card Number: 97-76261

ISBN: 1-56352-466-X

Digital film prep and imaging by Advertising Technologies, Inc., Atlanta, Georgia

Book design and typography by Martha Gill and Vivian Andres

TO MY LOVING HUSBAND,
DOUG SANDBERG,
BOTTOMS UP!

CONTENTS

modern
Cocktails
& Appetizers

RAISE YOUR GLASS – A few years ago, in the dead of winter, my husband and I found ourselves holed up in a Manhattan hotel room, waiting out the transition from late afternoon to early evening. It was too cold to shop. Too late for a museum. Too early for dinner. We sat in silence, vaguely restless. Then I gazed out of the window and saw, flickering in the cold twilight, a neon sign whose welcoming message succinctly announced the antidote to our mid-winter malaise: COCKTAILS. The bar itself turned out to be a dive, and by this time we were bent

A RITUAL STEEPED IN SPONTANEITY, FUN, ELEGANCE AND ROMANCE

on something more elegant. We trekked across the avenues to Rockefeller Center, took the elevator to the top and sat at the window in the Promenade Bar at the Rainbow Room. As we sipped a Sidecar and a Rob Roy, sampled tuna tartare and watched the snow swirl over the darkening city, I knew we had chosen how to spend our time wisely. ⬡ My husband and I are devoted to the cocktail hour. To us it means not only drinks, but delicious food and lively conversation as well. It is a ritual, steeped in spontaneity, fun, elegance and romance. The cocktail hour is a moment of anticipation, a time to dream of some grand possibility later in the evening. But it is also an experience unto itself, an interlude between day and night in which the energy from each meets and fuses into a wholly different sensibility, full of promise yet fleeting, like a sunset or a stolen kiss.   Like me, you have probably noticed the resurgence of the cocktail in the last couple of years. None too soon. At the time I was going to school in the late 1970s, and starting my career in the 1980s, my generation was celebrating not the cocktail hour, but the happy hour. The difference was more than seman-

THE DEMANDS OF MODERN LIFE CAN MAKE ENTERTAINING DIFFICULT

tic. With happy hour, getting drunk quickly and cheaply was the goal. Elegance was "stuffy." Cocktail fare meant bar snacks—pretzels, nuts, potato skins, chicken wings. And the classic Martini was shoved to the back of the bar, replaced by wine coolers, Jello shots, and awful drinks with frat house names that I won't repeat here.   Let's face it - something swank and swell had vanished. In fact, I'm convinced that a very important social safety valve disappeared from the American landscape during this bleak period, and with its passing came all sorts of nasty repercussions. (Who do you know who was really happy in, say, 1978 or 1989?) In the last few years, many of us have observed with pleasure as the cocktail has made a stunning comeback, bringing in its fizzy wake my two favorite sensibilities: elegance and fun. I believe the two need each other. Without elegance, fun becomes rough,

unbridled hedonism; without fun, elegance becomes cold and lifeless, the province of people with too much money and too little imagination. Together, they are a tonic. Make that a vodka tonic, with a twist.

THE COCKTAIL ESTHETIC – The revival of the cocktail hour stems, I believe, from a new attitude about entertaining and leisure time. People want the fun and informality of the '70s and '80s, but the elegance and sophistication of earlier times. What's more, they want to use their own creativity and their own style to make unique and memorable experiences—experiences that bring people together, excite their senses and offer all that is both simple and sublime. Still, the very real pressures of modern life can make entertaining difficult. So many of my friends tell me they long to entertain but keep putting it off because they don't have the

> BRING PEOPLE TOGETHER, EXCITE THEIR SENSES, OFFER THE SIMPLE AND SUBLIME

time. I fell into the same trap myself when my design business began taking off at the same time I had two children to take care of. Family came first. Career a close second. Friends and entertaining a distant third. Fortunately for my sanity, my husband and I recognized the growing insular pattern of our lives and determined to put a stop to it. Life should be more than work and domestic duties. It should have another dimension, another texture that needs careful attention and just a little bit of maintenance. Of course, the cocktail hour is just a small part of this sensibility. But it's not a bad place to start, because it begins to get at the larger picture of making life what it should be. Relaxed. Elegant. Spontaneous. Fun. *Modern.* And thus this book, which is really about nothing more complicated than having fun—without stress!

THE RULES OF ENGAGEMENT – Let's take the intimidation out of the cocktail hour. First, let's agree on a basic definition. To me, a cocktail is any drink that lifts the spirits or excites the palate. A cocktail can

YOU DON'T NEED A BAR CART FULL OF FRUITS, OLIVES, HERBS, AND VEGETABLES

mean a cold beer. A classic Martini. An exotic punch from Thailand. Or any drink that seems fun and right for the season or the moment. Alcohol certainly helps, and it is present in all the drinks in this book. But there are also delicious, alcohol-free cocktails you can find in any comprehensive bar guide. Choosing a cocktail should not be something you think too much about—it should be pleasurable and without second-guessing (you can always order another of something different). A few basic rules to guide us as we go forth: **Rule One:** There are no rules. This is about having fun. **Rule Two:** You don't need twelve kinds of glassware, twenty-three bottles of various spirits, or a bar cart full of fruits, olives, mint

leaves and three types of bitters. This is about simplicity. (See Stocking Up for the Cocktail Hour, page 97, for what

you *do* need.) **Rule Three:** You don't need to spend hours preparing appetizers or cocktails. This is about spon-

taneity. **Rule Four:** You don't need to have lots of people to enjoy the cocktail hour. My husband and

> A COCKTAIL CAN BE ANY DRINK THAT LIFTS THE SPIRITS OR EXCITES THE PALATE

I began our cocktail-hour odyssey by setting aside one day a week (not always a Friday or Saturday) for just the two

of us to meet at home at six sharp for drinks and appetizers. Once you get in the habit, it becomes easier to include

friends, colleagues and neighbors. This is about sharing the best of times.

PUTTING THIS BOOK TO WORK – Once you've achieved the proper frame of mind, infusing your life

with a splash of the cocktail hour will come easy. *Modern Cocktails & Appetizers* is here to help. Each chapter includes

one cocktail and one appetizer. But by all means feel free to mix things up a bit. Half the fun is bringing your own

creativity and style into the mix. The appetizers included here are exciting but simple,

easy to plan for and prepare. Most can be made in less than 30 minutes, and

we even include tips (see Stocking Up for the Cocktail Hour, page 97) for

keeping key ingredients on hand so you can serve something beyond Cheeze

Whiz and tortilla chips at serendipitous gatherings. We did, however, include a few more difficult recipes for special occasions. The Brandade and Potato Napoleon, for instance, is a delicious challenge, but we've simplified it to six steps, four of which can be done in advance. 🌼 Some of the recipes, on the other hand, are simplicity itself. For the ultimate in ease of preparation, choose the vodka and caviar. Make like Dr. Zhivago and Lara on a cold Siberian night, put on a sweater and build a fire. (Turn down the air conditioning to 58° if you must.) Pour vodka from the freezer and open a jar of caviar, nestle shot glasses and the caviar jar into a clear mixing bowl filled with ice and serve. You can

HALF THE FUN IS BRINGING
YOUR OWN CREATIVITY
AND STYLE INTO THE MIX

add red onions, capers or fresh chives—or not. Even without accompaniments, caviar will always be Czarishly decadent. (Warning: If you're not used to straight drinks, take it slow, or by the end of the night you'll be swearing that *you're* Anastasia.) 🌼 Finally, a quick word on supplies. Three types of glassware will suffice: a Martini glass, a tumbler, and a highball glass. Serve (what else?) Martinis in a Martini glass (also Cosmopolitans and other classic cocktails); Old Fashioneds, Gibsons, and just about anything over the rocks in the tumbler; and collinses, tonics, Bloody Mary's, and anything that seems better tall in the highball glass. For those of us who already have

them, balloon goblets are a good option for wine spritzers and Piña Coladas. (For more on supplies, see Stocking Up for the Cocktail Hour, p. 97.) ❁ So far, I've been easy-going and accommodating. I've avoided absolutes and dogma. But occasionally, modern means no compromises. And so it is with cocktail shakers. You need one, preferably with an ice strainer. Shaking drinks ensures proper mixing and chilling without spills or messes. Plus, the shakers themselves, with their sleek deco lines, are icons of twentieth-century design and look great sitting on the bar or even the kitchen counter. You'll feel like Myrna Loy as you gently shake the gin, vermouth and ice while winking slyly or snapping off a quick bit of wit to your own William Powell. ❁ Remember, above all, to think *modern*, and use your own creative spirit to enrich the cocktail hour or any occasion. I hope my ideas help. So have a cocktail. Try an appetizer. Enjoy the book. Enjoy your life.

Cheers—*Martha Gill*

"There's a gude time coming." —Sir Walter Scott, *Rob Roy*

Rob Roy

AND CARPACCIO CANAPÉS

– When the English stole his land, the dashing outlaw Robert MacGregor (aka Rob Roy, meaning, more or less, Robert the Red in Gaelic) took to the Scottish highlands, stole livestock and fought for justice. Sir Walter Scott immortalized him in his 1817 novel, Liam Neesam brought him to life in the 1995 film and this famous Scotch-based drink ensures that Rob Roy will have his name uttered thousands of times each week in bars around the world. Not a bad legacy for a cattle thief. Combined with the carpaccio canapés, this drink and appetizer duo makes for a thoroughly bold and British cocktail hour. Don't let carpaccio's Italian

> A TRULY HEROIC DRINK,
> AS ROUGH AND RUGGED AS
> THE SCOTTISH HIGHLANDS

name fool you. This dish is about beef and Stilton cheese, two flavors as British as the Union Jack or a pint of bitter at the corner pub. What's more, it's easy and quick to make, with no real cooking involved—just a few ingredients to combine and assemble. Have the butcher slice the sirloin very thin—one-sixteenth of an inch or so. Make the Stilton Cream the night before, and you can come straight home from work and straight into the mist-shrouded realm of a highland cocktail hour. If you're really pressed for time, skip the cream; instead, drizzle olive oil on the sirloin, then sprinkle grated Parmesan cheese and black pepper on top.

COCKTAIL – ROB ROY

- Splash of dry vermouth
- 1 1/2 ounces Scotch
- Dash Angostura bitters (optional)
- Cherry or lemon twist

Fill cocktail shaker with ice cubes. Pour a splash of dry vermouth onto the ice. Add Scotch, and, if desired, a dash of Angostura bitters, and shake. Serve straight up or on the rocks. Garnish with a cherry or lemon twist.

APPETIZER – CARPACCIO CANAPÉS

- 24 rounds of French bread or walnut bread
- 1/2 pound Stilton cheese, at room temperature
- 6 ounces cream cheese, softened
- 4 teaspoons whole-grain pommery mustard
- 1 teaspoon Worcestershire sauce
- 1/2 teaspoon freshly ground black pepper
- About 2/3 cup heavy cream
- 1 pound sirloin, sliced paper thin,* each slice wrapped in wax paper to prevent darkening
- Watercress sprigs, stemmed, washed, and patted dry

* Have butcher slice in 1/16-inch slices

Make the Toasts : Preheat the oven to 350°. Arrange bread rounds on a baking sheet and bake for 2 to 3 minutes, or until golden brown.

Make the Stilton Cream : In a food processor, pulse Stilton, cream cheese, mustard, Worcestershire, and pepper, adding cream a little at a time until mixture is of drizzling consistency. If desired, pour mixture into a plastic squeeze bottle.

Pipe or drizzle about $1/2$ teaspoon of Stilton Cream on each toast round. Arrange sirloin on top, top with additional Stilton Cream, and garnish with watercress.

Makes 24 canapés

In the 1930s, bar dice were a popular novelty—and a good way to win a free drink.

Substitute tile pieces for platters to create an original presentation.

Moscatto

Allegro

ON THE RIVIERA – The wine is Californian, but the soul of this combination lies somewhere between Portofino and Monaco, on the terrace of a villa perched above the azure waters of the Mediterranean. Moscatto Allegro carries just a hint of effervescence and can be served as a dessert wine or an aperitif. Here we simply pour it over the rocks and add a twist of lemon. The slight fizz gives the drink a cocktail feel, but it's lighter than a mixed drink and better than a wine spritzer. What could be more perfect on a sun-drenched afternoon? The trio of crostini are almost as easy to concoct as the drink. You can serve all three or pick your favorite. The ingredients store well and are easy to keep around the house, especially the cannellini beans and sun-dried tomatoes, making this appetizer one of the best selections for an impromptu gathering. Each of the three crostini has a distinct look, feel and flavor: The cannellini crostini is earthy and Tuscan; the Saga blue with grapes is sharper and more floral; the sopressata with artichoke is robust. The light frivolity of the wine complements each one, and together this cocktail and appetizer can help you carve out your own pleasant corner of la dolce vita.

A LANGUID COCKTAIL
HOUR WITH A
MEDITERRANEAN TWIST

COCKTAIL – MOSCATTO ALLEGRO

Serve chilled, over ice, with a lemon twist.

APPETIZER – CROSTINI TRIO

SOPRESSATA, PORT SALUT, AND ARTICHOKE

- 24 rounds of French bread
- 12 to 16 ounces Port Salut (semi-soft Italian cheese)
- 24 thin slices sopressata sausage, cut into $3/4$-inch strips
- 2 (6 ounce) jars of artichoke quarters, drained
- 2 teaspoons finely chopped lemon zest
- 2 tablespoons fresh basil leaves, cut in julienne strips

Preheat the oven to 350°. Arrange bread rounds on a baking sheet and bake for 2 to 3 minutes, or until golden brown.

Spread each toast with a teaspoon of Port Salut cheese. Top with a (looped-over) strip of sopressata. Add artichoke quarter and garnish with lemon zest and basil.

Makes 24 crostini

Serve in vintage glasses (like this one from the 1950s).

CANNELLINI WITH ROSEMARY AND SUN-DRIED TOMATOES

- 24 rounds of French bread
- 2 (16 ounce) cans of cannellini beans, drained
- About 1 cup extra-virgin olive oil
- $1/2$ cup sun-dried tomatoes, half cut in $1/4$-inch julienne strips and half cut in $1/2$-inch julienne strips
- $1/4$ cup chopped fresh rosemary

Preheat the oven to 350°. Arrange bread rounds on a baking sheet and bake for 2 to 3 minutes, or until golden brown.

Toss $1/2$ cup of cannellini beans in $1/4$ cup of the olive oil. Set aside. Mash remaining cannellini beans with a fork to a rough paste, adding enough of the remaining olive oil to make the paste spreadable and glistening. Season to taste with salt and pepper.

Spread each crostini with 1 teaspoon of bean paste. Top with a few of the whole beans and dot with sun-dried tomatoes. Garnish with rosemary and an additional grating of pepper.

Makes 24 crostini

THE SUN, THE SEA,
A SAIL IN THE DISTANCE,
A GLASS AT YOUR SIDE

Bar Tip: A twist is aptly named but often misused. Twisting the peel on the cocktail glass releases aromatic oils that enhance flavor. Simply tossing in a lemon peel will look pretty but do little else. So remember: Twist.

SAGA BLUE WITH GRAPES, FENNEL, AND CRACKED PEPPER

- 24 rounds of French bread
- 12 to 16 ounces Saga blue cheese
- 48 red seedless grapes, washed, patted dry, 24 halved
- 2 to 3 fennel fronds (do not wash)
- Coarsely ground black pepper

Preheat the oven to 350°. Arrange bread rounds on a baking sheet and bake for 2 to 3 minutes, or until golden brown.

Spread each crostini with a teaspoon of Saga blue cheese. Top with 2 grape halves and a whole grape. Garnish with a piece of fennel frond and finish with coarsely ground black pepper.

Makes 24 crostini

Mixing Music: French pop jazz vocalist Liane Foly sings chic ballads with just the right mix of romance, enui and sly sophistication.

Be gentle when muddling the mint; the goal is to release the oils but not the bitter, leafy taste.

Mint Julep

AND SMOKED TROUT PATÉ

A TRUE THOROUGHBRED – The Mint Julep. The Kentucky Derby. Was there ever a more symbiotic relationship between event and cocktail? Some 100,000 of these Bourbon-based drinks are served at the Churchill Downs racetrack during horseracing's biggest week, and countless more are concocted and consumed at Derby parties across the country. Sadly, this refreshing elixir—as much a part of the Southern mystique as Faulkner, Tara or Stonewall Jackson—all too often goes into a year-long hibernation until the horses gather in the paddock once more. But why wait? The Mint Julep, which dates to the late eighteenth century, has no rivals if you want a sophisticated cocktail

ON A HOT SOUTHERN NIGHT, THIS COMBINATION ALMOST BEATS AIR CONDITIONING

on a warm summer afternoon. The smoked trout paté continues the Southern theme, especially with its topping of peppered pecans. The taste is rich, earthy and addictive. Preparing the paté is quick and easy, but start it the night before so it can chill overnight. Keep a package of smoked trout in the freezer, and you can make this dish on short notice. Serve the paté on a cake plate, with lightly toasted rounds of French bread. Our version rejects the traditional silver cup in favor of clear glassware that allows the rich chestnut color of the Bourbon to shine through—like so many thoroughbreds churning around the final turn toward glory.

- Bunch of fresh mint sprigs
- 1 teaspoon superfine sugar
- Splash of water
- 1^1/$_2$ ounces Bourbon

Rub mint leaves around the inside of a cocktail glass, then place glass in the freezer for 30 minutes. In a small glass, gently muddle 2 or 3 mint leaves, superfine sugar, and a splash of water. Add Bourbon. Remove cocktail glass from the freezer and fill with crushed ice. Pour mixture over ice and stir until glass frosts. Garnish with sprigs of mint.

IN KENTUCKY, AFICIONADOS DEBATE THE FINE POINTS OF JULEP RECIPES

The Round Robin Bar in Washington's venerable Willard Inter-Continental Hotel is justly famous for its mint juleps.

- 1 pound cream cheese, brought to room temperature for a couple of hours
- 2 green onions, chopped (green plus 3 inches of white)
- 2 tablespoons plus 1 teaspoon fresh lemon juice
- 1 teaspoon grated lemon zest
- 1/4 cup fresh dill
- 1/4 teaspoon white pepper
- 1/4 teaspoon Tabasco
- 1 level tablespoon horseradish
- 12 ounces smoked trout
- Peppered Pecans

Pulse cream cheese in a food processor until smooth. Add green onions and pulse just until mixed and green specks appear. Add lemon juice, zest, dill, white pepper, Tabasco, and horseradish. Pulse to mix thoroughly.

SMOKED TROUT, TRULY ONE OF LIFE'S DELICATE AND DELICIOUS DIVERSIONS

Add trout in pieces to mixture and pulse to a rough paté. (Mixture should be thick.) Pack into a plastic-lined bowl, cover, and refrigerate overnight. Turn out onto a leaf-lined serving dish. Smooth surface with a spatula and garnish with Peppered Pecans and additional dill.

Mixing Music: "One mint julep was the cause of it all," laments Sarah Vaughan in her swinging 1954 song "One Mint Julep," which recounts how an innocent cocktail led to a shotgun wedding.

- $1/2$ to $3/4$ cup pecan halves
- 1 tablespoon butter
- $1/2$ teaspoon cayenne pepper
- 2 tablespoons plus 1 teaspoon brown sugar

Place pecans, butter, and cayenne pepper in a heavy skillet and sauté over medium heat until the nuts are browned. Add brown sugar and cook for 2 to 5 minutes, stirring constantly, until the sugar clings to the pecans. Allow pecans to cool, then chop. Sprinkle over Smoked Trout Paté

Serves 8 to 12

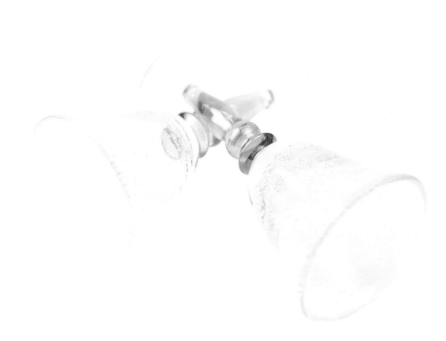

Use glassware that is fun and festive, whether it's Derby day or a mid-summer Monday.

Serve the Cosmopolitan in the same glassware you would use for a Martini.

Campari

Cosmopolitan

CAFÉ SOCIETY – On sidewalk terraces from Barcelona to Beirut, every other cafe umbrella seems to sport the alluring name of Italy's legendary aperitif: Campari. Created in 1861 by a Milanese bar owner named Gaspare Campari, this bitter, vivid red concoction is the quintessential European cocktail and a staple in classic drinks like the Negroni (see page 57) and the Americano. It's also good on the rocks, with a splash of Perrier. Here, we opt for something a bit stronger: a variation of the wildly popular Cosmopolotan with the Campari taking an edge off the sweetness and adding a subtle twist of Italian sophistication. The Mediterranean sampler features staples from the region—olives with garlic and rosemary, roasted red peppers, string cheese drizzled with olive oil. Each is quick and simple to prepare, and only the roasted red peppers require advance preparation. And if you use peppers from a jar, even that step can be eliminated, though you will lose a measure of flavor and texture. In addition, all the ingredients are easy to stock and store, allowing you to prepare a delicious and stress-free appetizer on the spur of the moment.

> CAMPARI, A BLEND OF BITTER, AROMATIC HERBS, IS EUROPE'S FAVORITE APERITIF

COCKTAIL – CAMPARI COSMOPOLITAN

- 1 $\frac{1}{2}$ ounces vodka
- 1 ounce Campari
- $\frac{1}{2}$ ounce lime juice
- 1 teaspoon superfine sugar
- 1 ounce cranberry juice
- Lime or lemon twist

Fill shaker $\frac{3}{4}$ full with ice cubes. Add all ingredients except twist and shake vigorously. Strain into cocktail glass, garnish with lime or lemon twist, and serve.

VARIATION –

Replace Campari with Cointreau for a classic Cosmopolitan.

APPETIZER – MEDITERRANEAN SAMPLER

HAYSTACK OF ARMENIAN STRING CHEESE

- 1 package (twisted rope) of Armenian string cheese
- $\frac{1}{4}$ cup extra-virgin olive oil
- 2 tablespoons roughly chopped fresh mint leaves
- 1 teaspoon grated lemon zest

Gently pull cheese apart, creating long, curly strings. Twist and lightly mound strings into a haystack. Drizzle with a little olive oil. Scatter mint leaves and lemon zest on top.

Serves 8

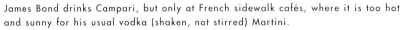 James Bond drinks Campari, but only at French sidewalk cafés, where it is too hot and sunny for his usual vodka (shaken, not stirred) Martini.

ROSEMARY AND GARLIC OLIVES

- 6 to 7 garlic cloves, peeled
- 1/3 cup extra-virgin olive oil
- 1 (16 ounce) jar medium to small green, cracked olives, drained and patted dry
- 1 tablespoon fresh rosemary leaves (leave whole)
- 1 tablespoon chopped fresh rosemary
- 1/4 teaspoon freshly ground black pepper

Slice 3 or 4 garlic cloves in half lengthwise. Leave remaining cloves whole. In a heavy saucepan heat olive oil over medium-high heat until almost smoking. Reduce heat to medium and add garlic. Stir to coat. Cook gently for 3 to 4 minutes.

Add olives to saucepan and continue cooking for 2 minutes. Add whole and chopped rosemary, toss to mix, and immediately remove from heat.

Toss with pepper and set aside at room temperature for 1 hour to meld flavors.

Serves 8

Mixing Music: Spin some Luscious Jackson, the hip, hard-edged, all-girl band from New York City that makes intelligent music you can actually dance to.

ROASTED RED PEPPERS

- 3 red peppers, cored, seeded, and cut into quarters
- $1/2$ cup extra-virgin olive oil
- $1/2$ cup fresh basil leaves, washed and patted dry
- Salt and freshly ground black pepper

Preheat broiler. Place peppers skin side up on a baking sheet or cake pan. Broil peppers, turning once, until they are blackened all over.

Remove from oven and place in a plastic or paper bag. Allow them to steam for 8 to 10 minutes. With a paring knife, scrape charred skin from peppers. (You may want to leave a little char for flavor.)

(Alternatively, use a jar of roasted peppers. Rinse with water, drain, and proceed with recipe as directed.)

Transfer a layer of peppers to a wide jar or small bowl. Drizzle with a little olive oil and top with a few basil leaves and a bit of salt and pepper. Repeat layering, cover, and refrigerate.

Bring to room temperature before serving.

Serves 8

 These bowls were designed to go on the nightstand, but work as well holding olives as they do spare change.

Caipirinha, meaning "farmers drink" in Brazilian slang, originated among the nation's sugar cane cutters.

Caipirinha

AND SPRING CRUDITÉS

TALL AND TAN AND YOUNG AND LOVELY – If she was old enough to drink, the Girl from Ipanema probably had a Caipirinha in her hand as she took her self-absorbed stroll to the sea, oblivious to the longing looks and choruses of "ahhhhs" emanating from the male populace along Rio's famed beach. The Caipirinha is virtually the national drink of Brazil, and in recent years it's gained great favor among the cocktail cognoscenti from West Hollywood to West Broadway. A distant cousin of the daiquiri, the Caipirinha gets its kick from Cachaça, the Brazilian spirit distilled from sugar cane juice. (Rum is distilled from the pulpy brown dregs left over when sugar cane

AN ENTICING BRAZILIAN ELIXIR, PERFECT FOR A LANGUID DAY AT THE BEACH

is turned to sugar; Cachaça lovers say the pure cane juice is a better base.) As in a Daiquiri, lime is a key ingredient, but instead of squeezing, you simply put a few wedges in the glass and muddle it with some sugar. Add the Cachaça and ice, and you have a delightful summer drink, just the cocktail for sunsets at sea or afternoons with your toes in the sand. The spring crudités are simple, healthy and fresh, served with a zippy tarragon sauce laced with Dijon mustard. Get creative with your cutting; if you have a French mandolin, carve your carrots into mod flame shapes.

COCKTAIL – CAIPIRINHA

- 1 lime, cut into quarters
- 1 teaspoon warm water
- 1 tablespoon superfine sugar
- 3 ounces Cachaça

Place lime quarters in bottom of glass. Add water and sugar and muddle together. Add 5 or 6 ice cubes and pour in Cachaça. Stir vigorously and serve.

APPETIZER – SPRING CRUDITÉS

MUSHROOMS TOSSED WITH SWEET ONION

- 1 pound domestic mushrooms
- 1 medium red onion, sliced into $1/4$-inch rings
- 9 whole bay leaves
- $1/2$ cup olive oil
- $1/4$ cup red wine vinegar
- 1 tablespoon lemon juice
- 1 teaspoon black pepper
- 1 teaspoon salt

Serves 8 to 12

Trim ends of mushroom stems. Slice larger mushrooms in half lengthwise. Place all ingredients in large bowl, toss, cover tightly, and refrigerate. Marinate for 2 to 4 hours, stirring occasionally. Serve with Lemon Tarragon Dip.

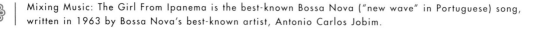

Mixing Music: The Girl From Ipanema is the best-known Bossa Nova ("new wave" in Portuguese) song, written in 1963 by Bossa Nova's best-known artist, Antonio Carlos Jobim.

BLANCHED SUGAR SNAP PEAS

- 1 pound sugar snap peas
- 1 tablespoon salt

Trim stem ends of sugar snap peas. Place in boiling salted water for 15 seconds. Immediately drain in colander and plunge into a bowl of iced water. Swirl around for 2 to 3 minutes to stop the cooking. Drain well and pat dry. Serve with Lemon Tarragon Dip.

Serves 8 to 12

Is this 1950s pig an early practitioner of the Macarena? You be the judge.

CARROT FLAMES

- 1 pound large, thick carrots, peeled

Wash carrots (do not trim). Slice lengthwise with a French mandolin to make furrowed, "flame" shapes, or slice carrots lengthwise with a sharp knife. Chill in iced water. Drain well and pat dry. Serve with Lemon Tarragon Dip.

SPRING CRUDITÉS ARE A HEALTHY ADDITION TO THE COCKTAIL HOUR

Serves 8 to 12

Lemon Tarragon Dip

- 3 tablespoons fresh lemon juice
- 3 tablespoons white wine vinegar
- 1 tablespoon coarse-grained Dijon or pommery mustard
- 1 teaspoon chopped fresh tarragon
- $1/2$ teaspoon sugar
- $1/4$ teaspoon salt
- Freshly ground black pepper
- $1/2$ cup safflower oil

Pulse all ingredients except oil together in food processor. With motor running, add oil gradually until incorporated. Chill until ready to serve. Gently whisk before serving.

Cachaça can be hard to find in the United States; if necessary, substitute light rum.

Let's get out of these wet things and into a dry Martini...

Classic Martini

DINO MEETS ZORBA — Sometime in the next century, cultural historians will no doubt gaze back on the 1990s and offer a plausible theory for the Martini craze that has so thoroughly swept the nation. Perhaps the real issue to ponder is why the drink fell out of favor in the first place. Almost since cocktails came into existence, the Martini has stood at the pinnacle of the genre, its very shape evoking all the heady elegance of the cocktail culture. Both real and fictional sophisticates always seem to have a Martini in their hands: Dorothy Parker. Nick and Nora Charles. Zelda Fitzgerald. Noel Coward. Cary Grant. James Bond. Unlike many drinks, the Martini has always been gender neutral—neither a "man's drink" nor a "woman's drink." And yet, the Martini hardly strikes an egalitarian posture, and in fact stands proudly for an elitism based not on money, but rather on good taste, sophistication and a certain joie de vivre. Of course, with the Martini now on the lips of the masses, one might suppose that its role as an icon of sophistication must necessarily end. If everyone's drinking them, can they still be that special? Our answer: Put some Dean Martin on the hi-fi and start mixing. Enlightenment (or at least a light head) will follow. While you're at it, make sure you have something to eat. (Martini Rule #1: Never have more than one on an empty stomach.) A trio of Greek-themed vegetarian spreads provides just the right hearty, straightforward flavors to stand up to a cocktail that (for all its polish) is still straight booze.

> THE HEADY SMELL OF GIN,
> A DASH OF VERMOUTH...
> ELYSIUM

COCKTAIL – CLASSIC MARTINI

- $^1/_2$ ounce dry vermouth
- $1\,^1/_2$ ounces gin
- Cocktail olive

Stir vermouth and gin in a pitcher filled with ice cubes. Strain into a chilled Martini glass. Garnish with an olive.

VARIATIONS –

- Dry: Use $1\,^2/_3$ ounces gin, $^1/_3$ ounce dry vermouth.
- Extra Dry: Swirl vermouth in glass and empty before adding 2 ounces of gin.
- Sweet: Use sweet vermouth.
- Vodka Martini: Replace gin with vodka. Replace olive with lemon twist.
- Tequila Martini: Replace gin with tequila.

APPETIZER – THREE VEGETARIAN SPREADS

FETA CHEESE AND OLIVE DIP

- $^1/_2$ cup softened cream cheese
- $^3/_4$ cup crumbled feta cheese
- $^1/_4$ cup sour cream
- $^1/_3$ cup pitted kalamata olives, some halved, some roughly chopped
- 2 tablespoons chopped fresh oregano
- 2 teaspoons grated lemon zest
- Freshly ground black pepper
- $^1/_3$ cup chopped roasted red peppers

For the full effect, serve your Martinis in a classic Martini pitcher, like this one from Barney's in New York.

In a food processor pulse the cream cheese, feta cheese, and sour cream briefly, retaining some of the bumpy texture of the feta.

Place cheese mixture in a bowl and stir in the olives, oregano, lemon zest, and black pepper. Gently fold in the roasted red peppers.

Serves 8

CUMIN-SCENTED HUMMUS

- 2 ($15^1/2$ ounce) cans chickpeas, drained (reserve liquid)
- $1/3$ cup tahini (sesame seed paste)
- $1/2$ cup extra-virgin olive oil
- 3 or 4 garlic cloves
- $1/3$ cup fresh lemon juice (2 to 3 lemons)
- 3 tablespoons ground cumin
- $3/4$ teaspoon salt
- $1/4$ cup reserved chickpea liquid
- 2 tablespoons chopped fresh parsley
- $1/2$ teaspoon paprika
- Additional extra-virgin olive oil

In a food processor process chickpeas, tahini, olive oil, garlic, lemon juice, cumin, and salt until smooth. Add only enough reserved chickpea liquid to make a thick, paste-like consistency. Remove to a bowl, sprinkle with parsley and paprika, and drizzle with a little olive oil. Taste for salt. Serve at room temperature.

Serves 8

How much vermouth? In the 1930s, Martinis were often half vermouth and half gin. Today, some bartenders use atomizers for just a trace of vermouth. Our advice: Experiment.

- 2 heads Belgian endive, leaves separated into "boats"
- 2 cups mayonnaise
- 3 garlic cloves, finely chopped
- $1/3$ cup breadcrumbs
- $1/4$ cup ground almonds
- 2 tablespoons chopped fresh parsley
- Salt and lemon juice to taste

Dip endive leaves in lemon juice to prevent browning. Set aside. Place all ingredients except salt and lemon juice in food processor. Pulse to a coarse mix. Do not puree. Taste for seasoning and adjust with a touch of salt and lemon juice.

Scoop a heaping teaspoon of the Skordalia onto each endive boat. Serve with Naan Crisps.

Serves 8

Naan Crisps

- 1 package naan bread or pita bread
- 2 to 3 tablespoons olive oil
- $^1/_4$ teaspoon sweet dried basil
- Salt and freshly ground black pepper

Preheat oven to 350°. Cut naan into triangles or wedges. Place on baking sheet. Brush with olive oil and sprinkle with dried basil and salt and pepper to taste.

Bake for 5 to 7 minutes, or until golden brown.

A classic Martini pitcher is not a must, but makes a groovy addition to the modern bar.

Bar Tip: Curaçao also comes in orange and red colors, so you can extend your Martini color palette to a warmer hue.

Blue Martini

AND DUCK BOBOLI

CHASE AWAY THE BLUES – Picasso had his Blue Period. Why shouldn't you? Blue, after all, is second only to black as the international color of cool sophistication. And cocktails are very much about cool sophistication. Turning a Martini (or any colorless drink) blue takes only a few dashes of blue Curaçao, the orange-flavored liqueur from the West Indies. The result is a vivid azure cocktail that looks like a little corner of the sea. Of course, the sweet Curaçao gives the Martini a wholly different taste, and purists might frown. But then, purists are always frowning, and how much fun is that? Boboli rounds are puffy, crusty, pizza-like disks available in most grocery stores. You can use them for all sorts of easy appetizers, so keep some on hand for impromptu gatherings (they freeze well). Here, we top the Boboli with Chinese barbecued duck, Gruyère and mozzarella cheeses, plum slices and wine-soaked cherries. You can find the duck already cooked at Asian markets or Chinese restaurants.

> A DASH OF CURAÇAO, AND YOUR MARTINI BECOMES THE WHOLE AZURE WORLD

35

COCKTAIL – BLUE MARTINI

- 2 ounces vodka
- Splash of blue Curaçao
- Orange or lemon twist

Fill a cocktail shaker with ice cubes. Add vodka and Curaçao and stir. Strain into a chilled cocktail glass and garnish with an orange or lemon twist.

APPETIZER – DUCK BOBOLI

- $^1/_4$ cup dried cherries
- $^1/_2$ cup plum wine
- 1 Chinese barbecued duck*
- 1 tablespoon sesame oil
- 1 tablespoon soy sauce
- 2 eight-inch Bobolis
- 2 ounces shredded mozzarella
- 8 ounces grated Gruyère cheese
- 1 fresh deep red or black plum, cut into $^1/_4$-inch crescent slices
- 1 scallion (top 3 inches of green only), thinly sliced on the diagonal
- 8 ounces Saga blue cheese, crumbled
- 2 tablespoons roughly chopped walnuts

*available in Asian markets

 Mixing Music: In 1957, tenor sax great John Coltrane recorded one of the masterpieces of modern jazz– "Blue Train." As serious cocktail music, it remains unsurpassed.

Two days before making the appetizer, soak the cherries in plum wine and allow to macerate.

Preheat oven to 375°.

Pull bite-sized pieces off the prepared duck. Be sure to include some crispy glazed skin.

Whisk sesame oil and soy sauce together and brush lightly over the Bobolis. Sprinkle on the mozzarella and top with Gruyère, leaving a 1/2-inch edge around the Bobolis.

Distribute the duck, plum slices, wine-soaked cherries, scallion, and Saga blue cheese evenly over the Bobolis. Top with walnuts. Bake for 5 to 7 minutes.

Serves 8 to 12

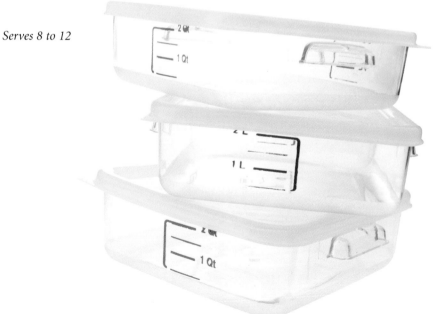

Use either vodka or gin in your Gibson—both are delicious.

Gibson

SWIMMING UPSTREAM – As sure as the noble salmon journeys far upstream to its birthplace to spawn and die, the Gibson aficionado keeps returning to this Martini variation, swearing (with some justification) that her chosen cocktail is more evolved than the original concoction. The argument is simple: Olives impart a nasty oily residue that defiles the gin or vodka. Substituting a cocktail onion (the only difference between a Martini and a Gibson) provides a cleaner, tastier garnish that preserves the true

TO SOME PURISTS, THE GIBSON OUTCLASSES EVEN THE VENERABLE MARTINI

character of the cocktail. (A twist of lemon is another option. But you can hardly eat a lemon peel, and for more than a few imbibers, whatever floats in the bottom of the glass constitutes a major food group.) The salmon skewers are a simple, elegant and delicious appetizer that requires no real cooking. The recipe calls for smoked salmon, which comes packaged and ready to eat. What could be simpler? Scottish salmon is our favorite, but there are other kinds on the market.

COCKTAIL – GIBSON

- Splash of dry vermouth
- 2 ounces gin or vodka
- Cocktail onion
- Lemon twist (optional)

Fill cocktail shaker with ice cubes. Add vermouth and gin or vodka and stir. Strain and serve straight up or on the rocks. Garnish with a cocktail onion and, if desired, a lemon twist.

APPETIZER – SALMON AND CUCUMBER RIBBONS

- 2 medium cucumbers
- 16 one-inch strips of Scottish smoked salmon
- 1 cup crème fraîche or sour cream
- $1/4$ cup fresh dill, stemmed and finely chopped
- 1 tablespoon finely diced red onion
- 1 tablespoon chopped fresh chives

Using a mandoline or very sharp knife, slice cucumbers lengthwise into 16 ribbons measuring about $1/8$-inch thick. Lay smoked salmon strips on top of cucumber ribbons and thread onto bamboo skewers.

Mix crème fraîche or sour cream with dill. Spoon into serving dish and scatter red onions and chives over the top.

Makes 16 skewers

 Mixing Music: Chet Baker, the jazz trumpeter with matinee idol good looks, helped create the cool West Coast sound in the 1950s.

Vivid Floribbean colors and flavors define this beautiful appetizer.

Daiquiri

WAR IS HELL — When the United States whipped up on Spain in the Spanish-American war of 1898, three valuable possessions were added to the burgeoning U.S. empire: the Philippines, Puerto Rico and the Daiquiri. In the aftermath of the conflict, a few U.S. mining engineers sent to a remote iron-ore mine in the Cuban town of Daiquiri unearthed something even better than pig-iron: this delightful drink featuring the local spirit of choice, light rum. A century later, it remains a cocktail classic—whether straight up, frozen or in infinite variations of fruit. The original version (and our choice) is, like most classic cocktails, a study in simplicity: lime juice, powdered sugar (or sugar syrup) and light rum. Mix one up, and remember the Maine! Our appetizer is a delicious challenge, and continues the Latin American theme. The tricky part is the glaze, a mixture of honey, lime juice, tequila and chipolte peppers that requires a good bit of time to reduce. To simplify, simply serve the shrimp with the avocado sauce and skip the corn griddle cakes. This is an ideal dish for a late summer barbecue, a last fling before fall returns and brings with it a more hectic pace.

> THE DAIQUIRI, A CLASSIC COCKTAIL, CELEBRATES ITS CENTENNIAL IN 1998

COCKTAIL – DAIQUIRI

- Juice of 1 lime
- 1 teaspoon superfine or powdered sugar
- 1 1/2 ounces light rum
- Lime wedge

Fill cocktail shaker with ice cubes. Add lime juice, sugar, and rum and shake. Strain into glass with ice cubes. Garnish with lime wedge.

VARIATION – FROZEN

- 1 1/2 ounces light rum
- 1 tablespoon triple sec
- 1 ounce lime juice
- 1 teaspoon superfine sugar
- 1 lime wedge

Place 5 or 6 ice cubes in a blender. Add all ingredients except lime wedge. Blend, pour into glass, and garnish with lime wedge.

APPETIZER – TEQUILA-GLAZED SHRIMP

- 24 large shrimp, peeled and deveined
- Tequila Glaze
- Avocado Cream
- Blue Corn Griddle Cakes
- Grated zest of 1/2 orange, plus a few curls
- Chopped cilantro

Frozen, on the rocks or straight-up, the Daiquiri is a refreshing drink that is perfect for a warm summer evening.

Tequila Glaze

- ¼ cup bottled Key lime juice, such as Nellie & Joe's
- ¼ cup tequila
- ¾ cup honey (orange blossom or other mild type)
- 1 teaspoon seeded and diced chipolte peppers

In a heavy saucepan stir together lime juice, tequila, and honey. Bring to a boil. Lower heat and cook until mixture has reduced almost by half and is syrupy.

Add chipoltes and cook for 2 to 3 minutes. Taste for heat. If peppers are too hot, pour glaze through a strainer to remove peppers and return mixture to saucepan. Continue to cook until glaze is the consistency of molasses. Taste, adding more honey or lime juice if necessary. Remove from heat. Glaze will thicken as it cooks.

Avocado Cream

- 1 medium avocado, preferably Haas
- ¼ cup crème fraîche or sour cream
- Salt
- Key lime juice

Puree avocado in food processor or blender. Scrape into a small bowl and fold in crème fraîche or sour cream. Add salt and lime juice to taste. Chill.

Keep an eye out for a classic cocktail mixing glass, complete with easy-to-follow instructions, at antique stores and thrift shops.

Blue Corn Griddle Cakes

- 1 cup blue cornmeal
- 1 cup all-purpose flour
- $1/2$ teaspoon baking powder
- $1/4$ teaspoon salt
- $1/4$ cup honey
- 2 eggs, lightly beaten
- $1 1/4$ cups milk
- 2 tablespoons melted butter
- $1/2$ teaspoon butter or vegetable oil for the griddle

Combine cornmeal, flour, baking powder, and salt in a medium bowl. In a separate bowl whisk together honey, eggs, milk, and melted butter. Add to dry ingredients and mix briefly.

Heat frying pan or griddle and add butter or vegetable oil. Drop batter onto pan to form small cakes about the size of half dollars. Cook over medium heat, turning once, until cakes are lightly browned on each side.

Assembly

Prepare a charcoal grill or broiler. Brush shrimp with cooled Tequila Glaze. Grill or broil shrimp until tails are crisp and shrimp turns pink, about 2 to 3 minutes.

Dollop each griddle cake with Avocado Cream. Top with shrimp and sprinkle with a little orange zest and chopped cilantro.

Makes 24 appetizers

When making Daiquiris, use fresh lime juice, never bottled. Strain the seeds and pulp through a fine strainer.

Mixing Music: Ella singing Duke Ellington. Ella singing Cole Porter. Ella singing anything.

Manhattan

NEW YORK, NEW YORK – In the 1930s, with Prohibition mercifully ended and cocktails back on the right side of the law, the Manhattan ranked second only to the Martini in popularity among the guys and dolls of New York. Forged from two strong spirits (whiskey and vermouth), it was a heavy drink for heavy times (this was, after all, the Great Depression). The Manhattan remained a standard until the 1970s, when Americans began turning away from hard liquors, especially whiskey. Even today, in the great Cocktail Comeback of the 1990s, the proud Manhattan seems overlooked. Which is a shame. If the Martini is Cary Grant, then the Manhattan is Humphry Bogart—a bit tougher, a tad less sophisticated, yet still very much in the province of the social elite. In fact, according to bartender lore, the Manhattan first came to life amid the dark wood and hunting prints of the Manhattan Club, where prominent and duly social-registered New Yorkers spent their old money keeping each other company. The impressive-looking Brandade and Potato Napoleon, with its rich fusion salt cod, garlic, heavy cream and potatoes, is a fitting companion to the Manhattan, and an ideal choice for a cool night.

> THE BRANDADE AND POTATO NAPOLEON IS IMPRESSIVE, BUT EASIER THAN IT LOOKS

COCKTAIL – GIBSON

- 1 $^{1}/_{2}$ ounces Canadian whiskey, Bourbon, or rye
- $^{1}/_{2}$ ounce sweet vermouth
- Maraschino or fresh cherry
- Orange slice (optional)

Fill cocktail shaker with ice cubes. Add whiskey, Bourbon, or rye and vermouth and shake. Serve straight up or on the rocks. If you serve on the rocks, use the same ice. Garnish with cherry and, if desired, orange slice.

APPETIZER – BRANDADE AND POTATO NAPOLEON

- 1 pound boneless, skinless salt cod
- 5 Idaho potatoes
- $^{1}/_{2}$ cup olive oil
- 7 or 8 garlic cloves, finely chopped
- $^{1}/_{2}$ teaspoon white pepper
- About $^{1}/_{2}$ cup heavy cream
- Salt and freshly ground fresh rosemary
- 2 teaspoons grated lemon zest
- Rosemary sprigs

The day before serving, cover the cod with cold water and soak overnight in refrigerator, changing water once. Drain, put in suacepan, add enough fresh water to cover, and bring to a boil. Reduce heat and simmer until tender, about 12 minutes. Drain well. Flake fish and remove any dark skin.

You can adjust the vermouth to concoct subtly different Manhattans. A traditional Manhattan uses sweet vermouth. Dry vermouth renders a Dry Manhattan. Equal parts of each delivers a Perfect Manhattan.

In a saucepan cover 2 potatoes with salted water and bring to a boil. Reduce heat and cook until potatoes are tender. Drain, peel potatoes, and mash.

In a skillet heat 2 tablespoons of the olive oil over medium heat. Sauté garlic until tender but not brown.

Place cod, mashed potatoes, white pepper, and garlic in food processor. Pulse, slowly adding heavy whipping cream until the texture resembles heavy (not stiff) whipped cream. At this point the brandade may be refrigerated for 2 to 3 days prior to serving.

Preheat oven to 375°. Peel remaining 3 potatoes and cut in $1/2$-inch slices. (You should have 6 to 8 slices per potato.) Brush with olive oil and sprinkle with salt and pepper to taste and chopped rosemary. Bake, turning once, until slices are brown, about 15 minutes. Remove from oven.

Reheat brandade in a suacepan, adding additional olive oil and cream to create a smooth, heavy sauce. Place potato slice on a warm plate and ladle with a little of the brandade. Repeat twice to create a "napoleon" of three layers. Repeat with remaining potato slices and brandade. Garnish with lemon zest and sprigs of rosemary.

Makes 6 to 8 napoleons

Bar Tip: To update this classic just a little, try using a fresh cherry instead of a Maraschino cherry.

Serve the Thai sauté in the cabbage boats or, for a more casual setting,
use the cabbage to scoop directly from the bowl. Hey, you're among friends!

Imported Beers

AND THAI BEEF SAUTÉ

EAST IS EAST – In far-off Bangkok, as in much of Asia, the drink of choice is clean, crisp beer served icy cold. Asian beers, especially those from Japan and China, are growing in popularity throughout America. Thai beers, like Singha, are equally good, though often hard to find outside Thai restaurants, Asian food markets or extremely well-stocked liquor stores. Thai cuisine, on the other hand, seems to be everywhere these days, both in restaurants ranging from sleek to homey and on supermarket shelves selling Thai ingredients. Our Thai Beef Sauté includes many of the ingredients that are hallmarks of exotic food from the beguiling land once known as Siam. Ginger. Cilantro. Garlic. Peanuts. And, of course, hot chili sauce (go easy). The feeling, and the flavors, are relaxed and casually elegant—all part of the modern esthetic which owes much to Asian design, culture and philosophy.

IT'S NOT REALLY A COCKTAIL, BUT BEING MODERN REQUIRES A FLEXIBILITY OF SPIRIT

COCKTAIL — IMPORTED BEERS

- Singha
- Kirin
- Tsing-Tao
- Sapporo
- Asahi

Serve well chilled.

 Bar Tip: For really cold beer really fast, toss a few handfuls of rock salt into a bucket of ice containing the beer bottles, and chill the glasses for 20 minutes in the freezer.

- 2 teaspoons vegetable oil
- 5 cloves garlic, finely minced
- 1 pound ground beef (chuck)
- 1 1/2 tablespoons naam pla (bottled fish sauce)
- 1/4 cup fresh lime juice
- 2 1/2 tablespoons sriracha chili sauce (bottled hot sauce)
- 2 scallions (white and 3 inches of green), thinly sliced diagonally
- 1 teaspoon sugar
- 2 teaspoons soy sauce
- 4 teaspoons fresh ginger, peeled and minced
- 1/2 cup roughly chopped fresh cilantro
- 1/3 cup finely chopped dry roasted peanuts
- Whole cilantro leaves for garnish
- 1 head green cabbage, halved and each half cut into thirds
  to form crescents

In a skillet over medium heat, heat vegetable oil until hot. Sauté garlic for 4 minutes. Add ground beef and toss until just cooked through. Remove from heat. Drain oil from skillet by patting with paper towels.

Place meat mixture in a large bowl and add remaining ingredients except peanuts, cilantro leaves, and cabbage. Mix well. Garnish with peanuts and cilantro leaves. Serve slightly warm, with cabbage crescents.

Serves 8

Making this Thai Beef Sauté is just a bit harder than making Hamburger Helper.

The glassware from Target is simple and affordable—just right for guests
with low tolerance or poor motor skills. Why risk the Waterford tumblers?

Vodka

Negroni

THE MEAN REDS – Like a grand and fiery sunset, the pinkish-red Negroni cocktail is the sort of drink that restores one's faith, or at least helps chase away the blues and other dark moods. As with Martinis, vodka seems (in our humble opinion) a better base than gin in a Negroni. With vodka, the drink loses its medicinal undertones, and the bittersweet blend of Campari and sweet red vermouth comes forth. These two vivid red spirits give the Negroni a rosy, almost psychedelic hue, not unlike the bubbling contents of those infamous lava lamps that are (like everything else) back in vogue again. The stuffed figs combine two of Italy's most sublime flavors—sharp, biting Gorgonzola cheese, and thin, delicate prosciutto. This appetizer is simple to make, and the end product has the trippy look of a dish you might have been served at an Andy Warhol party, circa 1967. But we guarantee: no flashbacks.

DROP IN, TURN ON, TUNE OUT, MIX GENTLY; THE NEGRONI IS ONE TRIPPY DRINK

COCKTAIL - VODKA NEGRONI

- 1 ounce vodka
- $^1/_2$ ounce Campari
- $^1/_2$ ounce sweet vermouth
- Splash of Perrier (optional)
- Lemon twist

Fill cocktail shaker with ice cubes. Add vodka, Campari, and vermouth. Stir and strain into glass over ice cubes. Add optional Perrier. Garnish with lemon twist.

APPETIZER - STUFFED FIGS

- $^1/_2$ cup diced ($^1/_4$ inch) fresh cantaloupe
- $^1/_2$ cup good-quality sweet vermouth
- $^2/_3$ cup Gorgonzola cheese, at room temperature
- $^1/_3$ cup ricotta cheese, at room temperature
- $^1/_2$ teaspoon finely grated orange zest
- 16 fresh Adriatic figs (green-skinned), washed and patted dry
- 16 thin strips of prosciutto
- 1 small bunch field greens

 Mixing music: Hendrix. Donovan. The Velvet Underground. And anyone doing a cover of "Crimson and Clover."

Marinate cantaloupe in vermouth for 1 hour at room temperature.

Preheat oven to 375°. In a small bowl, fold softened cheeses and orange zest together. Cut a stemmed "hat" off the top of each fig and set aside. Scoop a generous spoonful of flesh from each fig and stuff hole with cheese mixture.

Securely wrap the prosciutto around the outside of each fig. Bake for 8 to 9 minutes, or until the filling is bubbly and heated through.

Place a few field greens on each plate or on one large platter. Center figs. Scatter the diced cantaloupe and a few drops of the vermouth around the figs. If you like, replace the stemmed "hats." Serve immediately.

Makes 16 appetizers

Both the cocktail and the appetizer use sweet red vermouth.

Mixing Music: Try Tito Puente, one of the great stars of Mambo music.

Piña Colada

AND BAGS OF NIBBLES

CONGA LINE – Despite the sappy '70s song and the sickly-sweet supermarket mixes, the Piña Colada remains the undisputed El Presidente Por Vida of tropical cocktails. Properly made, it's one of the best tastes you can put in your mouth—a perfect blend of three components (rum, coconut and pineapple) that sum up the allure of the tropics better than swaying palm trees or white-sand beaches. Essentials for a great colada are fresh pineapple, cream of coconut and a quality rum, like Bacardi or Mount Gay. In other words, what you toss in the blender matters, and that's why this is one drink that should be better made at home than in most bars. The bags of nibbles may be the quickest and simplest appetizer in this book. The most complicated step is punching a few holes in the lunch bags and threading raffia through them. (You can use bowls instead, but remember that bags mean no clean-up.) Nuts, dried mango and other dried fruit echo the tropical feel of the cocktail. Use the time you save on this simple appetizer to shop for interesting glassware, like the tortoiseshell tumblers shown here.

IN THE VAST REALM OF TROPICAL DRINKS, THE PIÑA COLADA HAS NO EQUAL

COCKTAIL – PIÑA COLADA

- 1 1/2 ounces light rum
- 2 tablespoons cream of coconut
- 1/4 cup fresh pineapple
- 1 tablespoon toasted shredded coconut (optional)

Combine rum, cream of coconut, and pineapple with 5 or 6 ice cubes in a blender. Blend to a fine consistency and pour into glass. Garnish with toasted coconut.

APPETIZER – BAGS OF NIBBLES

- Turkish dates
- Dried fruit (mangos, pears, apples, figs)
- Raw sunflower or pumpkin seeds
- Cashews, Brazil nuts
- Nori maki rice crackers, wasabi, or sea vegetable chips

Use 4 or 5 standard-sized lunch bags. Choose one or all of the following options for decorating the bags (refer to photo opposite for guidance): 1) Fold top bag edges down twice. Using a hole punch, punch holes along the top edge of the bag, about 1/4- to 1/2-inch from top. Thread colored raffia through holes to "sew" the bag edge. 2) Fold top bag edges down twice. Punch two holes in the bag's two short sides. Thread colored raffia through the holes and tie in a bow. 3) Make a series of decorative cuts at top of bag. Fold bag back slightly at cuts. Fill bags with nibbles.

 Tip for blender drinks: Mix for 10 seconds at low speed, then for 10 more seconds at high speed.

The classic Whiskey Sour uses blended American whiskey or Canadian whisky, although some bars use Bourbon.

Whiskey Sour

SASSY – It's a state of mind. A bit of flirtatious irreverence. A point at which you speak your mind, push the limits of propriety and laugh at the consequences. You may stir something up. And while you're at it, you may as well stir up a Whiskey Sour (or a Rum Sour, a Vodka Sour, a Bourbon Sour or a sour made with just about any hard liquor you have in the cabinet above the kitchen sink). The Whiskey Sour is a sassy throwback, the sort of drink your mother might have drunk when courting back in the '50s. If

> CAN YOU TIE THE STEM OF A CHERRY IN A KNOT WITH YOUR TONGUE?

you're in the right age bracket, you may have had one or two as a teenager yourself, thanks to the fake i.d. your boyfriend's older sister procured for you. Well, it's high time to turn back the clock and try a Whiskey Sour again. Still has the same kick, the same lemon-citrus taste, the same Maraschino cherry. The spicy shrimp is easy to prepare. You can even marinate using store-bought mojo marinade. So go forth. Life is short. Be sassy.

COCKTAIL – WHISKEY SOUR

- $^1/_2$ ounce lemon juice
- $^1/_2$ teaspoon superfine sugar
- $1^1/_2$ ounces blended whiskey
- Maraschino cherry
- Orange or lemon slice

Combine lemon juice, sugar, and whiskey in a cocktail shaker filled with ice. Strain into glass with ice cubes or shaved ice. Garnish with cherry and orange or lemon slice.

VARIATIONS – SUBSTITUTE FOR WHISKEY

- Rum Sour: $1^1/_2$ ounces rum
- Vodka Sour: $1^1/_2$ ounces vodka
- Tequila Sour: $1^1/_2$ ounces tequila
- Bourbon Sour: $1^1/_2$ ounces Bourbon
- Scotch Sour: $1^1/_2$ ounces Scotch

 These serving bowls come from a Chinese hardware store in San Francisco.

APPETIZER – SHRIMP WITH SALSA VERDE

- 32 large shrimp, peeled and deveined
- 1 cup bottled mojo marinade
- Salsa Verde
- Red, yellow, and blue corn chips (optional)

CHANCES ARE, YOU HAD
A WHISKEY SOUR
ON PROM NIGHT

Marinate the shrimp in mojo for 1 hour in the refrigerator. Preheat the grill or broiler. Grill or broil shrimp until just pink and tails are crisp.

Spoon mounds of Salsa Verde onto an attractive platter or individual serving plates or bowls. Arrange shrimp tail-up on salsa and serve with corn chips. If you like, provide small bamboo picks for skewering the shrimp.

Serves 8 to 12

Mixing Music: sassy sambas from Stan Getz and Jao Gilberto.

Salsa Verde

- 1 cup store-bought salsa verde (medium heat)
- 3 tablespoons frozen pineapple juice concentrate
- 1 $1/2$ tablespoons fresh lime juice
- $1/3$ cup finely diced red onion
- $1/8$ to $1/4$ teaspoon habanero pepper sauce
- 1 tablespoon honey
- $1/2$ cup diced ($1/4$ inch) fresh tomatillos
- 1 to 2 tablespoons chopped fresh cilantro

While the shrimp are marinating, combine all salsa ingredients except cilantro in a bowl. Stir gently and set aside for at least 1 hour to meld flavors. Garnish with cilantro.

 The classic silver cocktail shaker can't be beat, but brightly colored versions make occasional fun substitutes.

Mixing music: Royal Crown Revue, perhaps the best of the new generation of swing bands.

Sazerac

AND CHEESEBALLS

LIFE WITH A TWIST — To take the old and make it not just new, but better than the original—there is the great challenge for the modern esthete. Operating on the assumption that everything has been done before, we can still look to the past for inspiration, and search for ways to upgrade the retrograde. With cheeseballs, this is pretty easy. They weren't all that good to start with, consisting usually of processed cheese spread and stale nuts. Replacing these with a few higher-end ingredients yields a delightfully resurrected appetizer. The next challenge: Find and update the cocktail equivalent to the cheeseball. Our solution was to take the simple Old-Fashioned, a blend of whiskey, bitters and sugar cube, and turn it into the très chic Sazerac by adding a splash of Pernod. The sophisticated aniseed-flavored spirit from France imbues the drink with a freshness and complexity worthy of a young Belmondo.

> IT'S TIME TO REVAMP THE CHEESEBALL, A STANDARD AT MOM AND DAD'S PARTIES

COCKTAIL – SAZERAC

- 1 sugar cube
- Dash of Angostura bitters
- 1 $1/2$ ounces whiskey
- $1/4$ ounce Pernod
- Splash of water or club soda (optional)
- Orange or lemon slice

THE SAZERAC IS
A DASHING AND SNAPPY
COCKTAIL THAT TINGLES

Saturate sugar cube with bitters. Place in glass and crush with the back of a spoon. Add ice cubes, then whiskey and Pernod. Top with water or soda, if desired, and garnish with orange or lemon slice.

 The undulating glassware is from Moss in New York City's Soho.

Appetizer – Cheeseballs

- 8 ounces Port wine cheddar
- 4 tablespoons butter
- $1/4$ teaspoon Worcestershire sauce
- 2 tablespoons tawny port or sweet sherry
- $3/4$ cup all-purpose flour, measured then sifted
- 30 large stuffed cocktail olives
- $1/2$ cup walnuts, toasted and roughly chopped
- Grated zest of 1 orange

In food processor process cheese with butter until light and fluffy. Add Worcestershire, port or sherry, and flour. Pulse to a stiff dough. Chill, covered, for 1 hour.

Preheat oven to 375°. Shape dough around olives to form 1- to 1 $1/2$-inch balls. Roll balls in toasted walnuts. Place balls on baking sheet and bake for 12 to 15 minutes. Garnish with a scatter of orange zest.

Makes 30 small cheeseballs

From Marseille to Montmartre, Pernod mixed with water is the cocktail of choice among the beret-clad elderly gentlemen of France.

"Oh, I wish I was in the happy land, where the river of brandy flows..."

Grappa

Sidecar

SCIENCE PROJECT – Ah, the thrill of discovery. A few C.C.s of this. A few M.L.s of that. And poof! Smoke billows forth in thick white clouds, and when it clears you've won the Nobel Prize for chemistry. Such was the dream of many a pocket protector-wearing kid with a Bunsen burner from Boise to Biloxi. Well, here's our second chance. We're all grown up now, and our assignment is to concoct the perfect cocktail—in this case, the perfect Sidecar. But there's a twist: Instead of the usual brandy, we'll use grappa, the fiery Italian spirit distilled from the skins and stems of grapes. It renders a lighter-colored Sidecar with a cleaner, more neutral taste. The cheese tortellini is more art than science, though you might accuse us of forgery after whipping up the "cheating" aioli. Use store-bought mayonnaise, but no light or nonfat brands, please! (We may cheat a bit, but we still have standards.) This saves you the tedium of separating egg yokes and allows you to spend more time in the laboratory. But be careful. Remember what happened to Dr. Jekyll.

> TURN A COLANDER UPSIDE DOWN TO CREATE AN IMPROMPTU SERVING DISH

COCKTAIL – GRAPPA SIDECAR

- $3/4$ ounce lemon juice
- $1/2$ ounce triple sec
- $1 1/2$ ounces grappa

Fill cocktail shaker with ice cubes. Add ingredients and shake well. Strain into glass filled with ice cubes.

VARIATION –

Replace grappa with 1 $1/2$ ounces of Cognac or brandy.

APPETIZER – CHEESE TORTELLINI

- $1/3$ cup olive oil
- 1 teaspoon finely minced garlic
- $3/4$ tablespoon sweet dried basil
- 1 scant teaspoon freshly ground black pepper
- 1 (9 ounce) package fresh or frozen plain tortellini, defrosted
- 1 (9 ounce) package fresh or frozen spinach tortellini, defrosted
- Sun-Dried Tomato Aïoli

Heat olive oil in a sauté pan over medium heat. Sauté garlic until just translucent, 1 or 2 minutes. Transfer garlic and oil from pan to a large bowl. Add basil and pepper and whisk together.

 Grappa was one of the many drinks associated with the literary lion of the cocktail, Ernest Hemingway.

Cook tortellini according to package directions. Rinse in cold water and drain. Add tortellini to bowl and gently toss to coat. Tortellini can be prepared the day before. Cover, chill, and bring to room temperature before serving. Serve with Sun-Dried Tomato Aïoli. Provide fondue forks or small picks for dipping.

Sun-Dried Tomato Aïoli

- $1/4$ cup sun-dried tomatoes, drained and patted dry
- $1 1/2$ teaspoons finely minced garlic
- $1/4$ cup freshly grated Parmesan cheese
- $1/8$ teaspoon freshly ground black pepper
- $1 1/2$ cups good-quality mayonnaise
- Parmesan shavings
- 3 tablespoons roughly chopped fresh basil

In a food processor blend sun-dried tomatoes, garlic, grated Parmesan, and pepper to a coarse consistency. Transfer to a bowl and clean the work bowl of the food processor.

In the food processor blend $1/4$ cup of the mayonnaise with 2 tablespoons of the sun-dried tomato mixture. Process to a rich, tomato-colored puree. Gently fold together the remaining mayonnaise with the remaining sun-dried tomato mixture. Fold in the puree from the food processor. Place in a serving dish and top with Parmesan shavings and chopped basil. Serve at room temperature.

Serves 8

A U.S. army captain stationed in Paris during World War I created the Sidecar at the famed Harry's New York Bar. A few of these, and getting back to the barracks meant riding in the motorcycle's sidecar.

Make your glassware as colorful as the drink.

Sangria

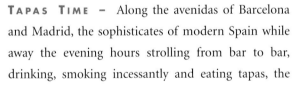

AND TURKEY MOLÉ TORTILLAS

TAPAS TIME – Along the avenidas of Barcelona and Madrid, the sophisticates of modern Spain while away the evening hours strolling from bar to bar, drinking, smoking incessantly and eating tapas, the delightful assortment of hors d'oeuvres that are so much a part of the Spanish sensibility. In more than a few of the clinking glasses you will find Sangria, a mixture of red wine, brandy and fresh fruit, served cold. It's delightful and festive, with the brandy providing an extra kick and the fruit permeating the drink with a citrus bouquet. Sangria is best when you allow enough time—at least an hour—for the fruit to thoroughly flavor the mixture. Use merlot or one of the plethora of inexpensive Spanish red wines on the market. The tortillas with turkey molé filling continue the Spanish theme, though in this case filtered through the prism of Spanish America. The thick, brown, pungent sauce known as molé is a staple of Mexican cooking. Here, we use it as a base to create a rich and exotic filling almost like chili. Use it as a dip or to fill tortillas, or eat right from the pot. Any way, you've just joined the tapas set.

A FUN-FILLED, FRUIT-FILLED COCKTAIL HOUR WITH SANGRIA AND TORTILLAS

COCKTAIL-SPANISH SANGRIA

- 1 bottle of Spanish wine, chilled
- 2 to 3 ounces brandy
- Assorted fresh fruits, such as oranges, lemons, limes, and pineapples, sliced thin

Combine all ingredients in a large pitcher and stir. Let stand at room temperature for at least 1 hour. Serve over ice or straight up.

APPETIZER-TURKEY MOLÉ TORTILLAS

- 1 medium yellow onion, minced
- 2 large garlic cloves, finely chopped
- 1 pound ground turkey
- 2 tablespoons chili pasa molida (dark ground chilies)*
- 2 cups canned Roma tomatoes with juice, roughly chopped
- 2 tablespoons tomato paste
- $1/8$ to $1/4$ teaspoon habanero pepper sauce
- $1/4$ cup prepared molé sauce (dark, rough texture)*
- 2 tablespoons dark Mexican cocoa (or Dutch-process cocoa)
- $1/4$ to $1/3$ cup currants
- 1 teaspoon ground cumin
- 1 cinnamon stick
- $1/2$ cup red wine (inexpensive burgundy or merlot)
- 1 pear or crisp apple, cut in $1/4$-inch dice
- $1/4$ cup roughly chopped toasted pumpkin seeds
- 2 tablespoons toasted sesame seeds

Available in the ethnic section of some supermarkets

In heavy pot sauté the onion, garlic, and ground turkey over medium heat until turkey is slightly browned. Add pasa molida and cook for a few more minutes.

Add the remaining ingredients except the pear or apple, pumpkin seeds, and sesame seeds. Stir to mix and simmer on low heat for 30 minutes.

When the mixture has reduced to a dark, aromatic molé, add the chopped fruit. Simmer until the fruit is softened.

Sprinkle with pumpkin seeds and sesame seeds and serve warm with corn chips, warm tortillas, wedges of lime, and crumbled queso blanco (white cheese).

Serves 8 to 12

In Spanish, *sangre* means blood—it doesn't take an etymologist to figure out how Sangria got its name.

Go ahead and mess with a good thing! The colorful stuffing and topping make this classic Brie even better.

Wine Spritzer

AND STUFFED AUSSIE BRIE

AUSTRALIAN FOR COCKTAIL – Cool, refreshing and simple, these wine coolers are a delicious and low-alcohol option for the cocktail hour. Start with one of the many excellent and inexpensive Australian Chardonnays now on the market. (You can, of course, use any Chardonnay or dry white wine.) Rosemount Estate and Oxford Landing are two reliable choices, but experiment a bit and find one you like. Then add a splash of Perrier and a slice of orange or lemon and serve in some inventive glassware, like the oversized wine glass shown on the next page. What do we mean by Aussie Brie? It's not the cheese that's Australian—it's the mixture lacing through the center that gives this appetizer a touch of down-under flair. Australia's lush subtropical regions produce an abundance of fruits, peppers and exotic produce, which we use here to make the Brie rich, sweet and pungent. All the ingredients keep well for easy and spontaneous preparation. You can make the entire appetizer ahead of time and freeze it—it will keep for about a month.

BRING YOUR GUESTS INTO THE KITCHEN AND PREPARE THIS DISH OVER DRINKS

COCKTAIL – WINE SPRITZER

- 4 to 6 ounces chilled Australian chardonnay
- 1 to 2 ounces Perrier or club soda
- Lemon wedge or twist

Combine the chardonnay and Perrier or club soda. Serve in a wine glass, with ice cubes if desired. Add a lemon wedge or twist.

APPETIZER – STUFFED AUSSIE BRIE

- 1 1/4 cups roughly chopped nuts (pistachios, pine nuts, walnuts, or pecans)
- 4 tablespoons (1/2 stick) unsalted butter
- 1/2 medium yellow onion (Walla Walla or Vidalia in season), diced
- 1 yellow pepper, cored, seeded, and finely diced
- 1 red pepper, cored, seeded, and finely diced
- 1 cup dried apricots, chilled, then diced
- 3/4 cup fresh basil leaves, lightly packed
- Splash Australian chardonnay
- 9-inch round of brie (may be slightly under 2 pounds)
- Toasted bread rounds

The chic, sophisticated alternative to the prepackaged wine cooler.

Preheat oven to 350°. Spread nuts on a baking sheet and toast until golden, about 7 minutes. Set aside.

In a sauté pan heat the butter over medium heat. Sauté onion and peppers until soft but not brown. Reduce heat, add apricots and basil, and sauté over medium-low heat for 4 to 5 minutes, stirring often.

Add toasted nuts to the pan and stir to mix. Add a splash of wine to deglaze the pan and cook briefly, stirring to coat fruit and vegetables with wine. Remove from heat and allow mixture to cool.

Heat a thin, sharp knife over a flame or run under hot water. Split brie horizontally. Spread fruit and nut mixture evenly on bottom layer, reserving 1/3 cup of mixture for top. Replace top layer of brie. (At this point, brie may be wrapped and frozen for up to 1 month.)

Top brie with remaining mixture. Heat briefly in microwave until edges of brie just begin to soften. Serve with toasted bread rounds.

Serves 8 to 12

Our serving tray comes from the shop at the Delano Hotel, in Miami's ultra-hip South Beach.

Get creative with the coatings —
bring your own style and taste to the table.

Bangkok

AND STICKY RICE BALLS

Punch

HOUSE RULES – In the golden age of cocktails, every swank boîte had its own house drink. Often, these libations were merely slight variations on the classics—a Martini with an extra ingredient, for example. A rare few are true originals that find their own place in the cocktail pantheon, like the Bellini from Harry's Bar in Venice or the famed "corpse revivers" from the Ritz Bar in Paris. We can't say what history will make of the Bangkok Punch created by inventive minds at Vong, a stylish New York restaurant that offers a mix of Thai and French cuisine. But we can say, with some authority, that it packs quite a wallop.

A GINGER INFUSION LACED WITH RUM, THIS EXOTIC PUNCH EVOKES THE ORIENT

Consider a few of the ingredients: ginger, Thai chile, lemongrass, cayenne pepper. This piquant concoction is the most time-consuming to prepare of any cocktail in this book. And you might have to hunt around for lemongrass stalks and Thai chilies, depending on where you live. But if you have the time and the patience, the rewards are worth it. The sticky rice balls are almost as fun to make as to eat, and are an excellent appetizer choice when guests will be helping you in the kitchen. We suggest several tasty coatings in which to roll the rice balls, but they also taste awfully good plain.

COCKTAIL – BANGKOK PUNCH

- 1 1/2 ounces Ginger Infusion
- 1 1/2 ounces dark rum
- 1 1/2 ounces papaya juice (or use pineapple or mango juice)
- 1/2 ounce lemon or lime juice
- Dash cayenne pepper
- Pineapple wedge

Mix all ingredients except cayenne pepper and pineapple wedge in a shaker and shake vigorously. Serve over ice and top with a dash of cayenne pepper. Garnish with a pineapple wedge.

Ginger Infusion

- 2 quarts water
- 1 cup sugar
- 3/4 pound fresh ginger, cut in pieces
- 1 stalk of lemongrass, cut in thirds
- 1 Thai chile, stemmed and seeded

Put water in stockpot and add sugar. Stir until sugar is dissolved. In a food processor pulse ginger, chile, and lemongrass until roughly chopped. Add mix to stockpot and bring to a boil. Boil mixture until it is reduced by half. Allow to cool. Strain mixture through fine sieve. Ginger Infusion will keep in the refrigerator for up to 2 weeks.

 Our thanks to Philipe Gouze, the manager at Vong in New York City, for the Bangkok Punch recipe.

APPETIZER – STICKY RICE BALLS

- 2 cups uncooked glutinous rice

FILLINGS

- Crab meat
- Avocado
- Pre-cooked tiny shrimp
- Jicama
- Cilantro
- Smoked scallops
- Fresh plums
- Enoki and shitake mushrooms
- Preserved ginger

COATINGS

- Snipped chives
- Toasted plain or black sesame seeds
- Brightly colored flying fish roe
- Black caviar
- Toasted pine nuts
- Chopped nori (thin sheets of dried seaweed)
- Chopped fennel tops

Rolling the rice balls is a tactile delight, making this recipe as much fun to make as it is to eat.

In a heavy-bottomed pot bring 3 cups of water to a boil. Add rice and return to a boil. Cook for 1 minute. Drain rice and return to pot. Cook, covered, over low heat for 20 minutes. Let stand, covered, for 10 minutes.

Choose a variety of fillings. Chop items into small pieces. Combine items according to taste. Some examples of good combinations: crab and avocado; baby shrimp, jicama, and cilantro; duck and plums; smoked scallops and preserved ginger.

Set out a bowl of warm water, a clean dishcloth for your hands, and a plate rubbed with oil. Moisten hands with warm water. Scoop about 1 to 2 tablespoons of rice, mold around a small amount of filling, and shape into a 1-inch ball between your palms. Set on oiled plate. Repeat with remaining rice, wiping your hands as needed.

Roll Sticky Rice Balls in the coatings of your choice. Set on a platter or tray. Serve with Dipping Sauce.

Serves 8

Mixing Music: Pop in the Pet Shop Boys. The upbeat tunes will keep you and your friends rolling.

Dipping Sauce

- $1/2$ cup seasoned rice vinegar
- 2 tablespoons sesame oil
- $1/2$ teaspoon chili oil
- 2 teaspoons low-sodium soy sauce
- $1/2$ teaspoon sugar
- 1 large scallion, cut into $1/2$-inch diagonal slices

Whisk together all ingredients except scallions. Pour into bowl and top with scallions.

WHAT COULD BE BETTER THAN SIPPING EXOTIC PUNCH WITH YOUR MOST EXOTIC FRIENDS?

Once you have mastered the rice balls, experiment with your own combination of ingredients.

Some of the best vodkas today come from Poland, including Wyborowa and Luksusowa, which is hardly surprising, since Poles (not Russians) invented the spirit in the late Middle Ages. The name derives from *woda*, the Polish word for water.

Vodka

TO THE HEALTH OF THE CZAR — If you weren't a serf, an oppressed worker or a radical on the wrong end of a Cossack saber charge, life in old Russia was one big rich bowl of borscht. A grand house on the Neva. Winters in sun-streaked Italy. Long weekends at a Dacha in the country. Glittering nights at the ballet and restful days by the fire reading Tolstoy (or lunching with him if you ran in the right circles). And each day was richly flavored by Russia's renowned refreshments—vodka and caviar. Despite war, revolution and official contempt for such capitalist pleasures, this sublime combination has survived the

ELEGANCE ON ICE, VODKA AND CAVIAR CAPTURE THE SPIRIT OF OLD RUSSIA

tumult of the twentieth century quite intact. Here, we suggest a few accompaniments—capers, red onions, chives—but you don't really need them. A note on caviar: It comes in lots of varieties, depending on the size and color of the roe and the type of fish from which it comes (the best are from sturgeon). Pictured here is a light gray Osetra, a delicate roe from Caspian Sea sturgeon. Domestic caviar is less expensive, but, as Comrade Lenin was fond of saying, "you get what you pay for." With both vodka and caviar, we advise unrestrained splurging. In short, live for the moment. Who knows when the next revolution might come?

COCKTAIL – VODKA

- 2 ounces high-quality vodka. We suggest Stolychnaya, Absolut, or Skye.

Serve very cold in a chilled shot glass.

APPETIZER – CAVIAR WITH ACCOUTREMENTS

- 1 hard boiled egg
- 2 slices of dark brot bread or pumpernickel
- 2 slices of good-quality white bread
- 1 ounce of caviar, such as beluga, sevruga, or malossol
- $^{1}/_{4}$ cup minced red onion
- $^{1}/_{2}$ cup crème fraîche or sour cream
- $^{1}/_{4}$ cup small capers
- $^{1}/_{4}$ cup snipped fresh chives
- 2 or 3 lemon wedges

Separate the yolk from the white of the egg. Force the yolk through a sieve and finely dice the white. Set aside.

Cut the dark bread into triangle wedges. Trim crusts from white bread and discard. Gently flatten bread with a rolling pin. Toast until golden and dry. Arrange caviar, red onion, crème fraîche, capers, chives, and lemon wedges in small bowls and nestle into ice-filled mixing bowl. Put chilled vodka and glasses in bowl, or arrange separately on a small tray.

Serves 2

Mixing Music: Rachmaninov's lushly romantic Piano Concertos Numbers 2 and 3.

With a little planning and purchasing, you can have a bar and pantry stocked with enough supplies to be well pre-pared for the cocktail hour. This guide includes the essentials for what you'll need to get started, but it is by no means a comprehensive list of equipment, liquors, mixers or food. Little by little, as you unearth new concoctions and dis-cover what you enjoy, you can add to the assortment. In general, spend more on premium brands when the spirit in question is one you tend to drink straight or (as with Martinis) diluted only by traces of other liquors. But if the liquor is for mixing, the choice is less important. In other words, the gin you put in a Martini is infinitely more important than the gin you put in a gin and tonic. Whatever your choices, find a liquor store with a knowledgeable staff, and have fun shopping.

BAR EQUIPMENT

Blender

Cocktail sticks/stirrers

Corkscrew

Ice bucket

Ice tongs

Jigger

Shaker with strainer

LIQUORS

Bourbon

Brandy

Campari

Canadian Whisky

Cointreau

Dry vermouth

Gin

Light Rum

Scotch

Tequila

Vodka

Mixers/Juices/Bitters

Angostura bitters

Cranberry juice

Gingerale

Lemon juice

Perrier

Orange juice

Rose's Lime Juice

Tonic water

Sweeteners/Spices

Black pepper

Cayenne pepper

Cream of coconut

Paprika

Salt

Sugar cubes

Superfine sugar

Tabasco

Worcesterchire sauce

Lemons

Limes

Maraschino cherries

Oranges

Pearl onions

Stuffed green olives

Assortment of nuts

Canned cannellini beans

Canned chickpeas

Canned Italian tomatoes

Cinnamon sticks

Currants

Dried apricots

Dried cherries

Dry roasted peanuts

Glutinous rice

Jar of roasted red peppers

Nori

Nori maki rice crackers

Pumpkin seeds

Sea vegetable chips

Sun-dried tomatoes (packed in oil)

Sunflower seeds

Tahini

Turkish dates

Horseradish

Molé

Naam pla fish sauce

Salsa verde

Soy sauce

REFRIGERATOR

Armenian string cheese

Assortment of black and green olives

Brie round

Capers

Cream cheese

Dijon or pommery mustard

Feta cheese

Mayonnaise

Parmesan cheese

Port wine cheddar

Sour cream or crème fraîche

FREEZER

Assorted breads: pita, brot, baguettes, Boboli rounds, naan

Ginger

Ground beef

Ground turkey

Prosciutto

Smoked salmon

Smoked trout

Sopressata sausage

Ad Hoc Softwares
410 West Broadway
New York, NY 10012
212/925-2652
(barware, glassware)

Anthropologie
375 West Broadway
New York, NY 10012
212/343-7070
215/564-2313 (for additional store locations)
(barware, glassware)

Antique Addiction
436 West Broadway
New York, NY 10012
212/925-6342
(vintage shakers, bar dice, glassware)

Baccarat, Inc.
625 Madison Avenue
New York, NY 10022
212/826-4100
800/777-0100 (for additional store locations)
(barware, glassware)

Banana Republic
2 Harrison Street
San Francisco, CA 94105
415/777-0250
800/333-7899 (for additional store locations)
(barware, glassware)

Barney's New York
660 Madison Avenue
New York, NY 10021
212/826-8900
800/822-7639 (for additional store locations)
(barware, glassware, linens, platters)

Bella Cucina Artful Food
800/580-5674 (for catalogue)
(gourmet foods, kitchenware)

Belle Chambre
321 Pharr Road, Suite F
Atlanta, GA 30305
404/816-5333
(linens)

Bridge Kitchenware
214 East 52 Street
New York, NY 10022
212/838-6746
(barware, glassware, kitchenware)

Broadway Panhandler
477 Broome Street
New York, NY 10022
212/966-3434
(kitchenware)

Calvin Klein Home
800/294-7978 (for nearest retailer)
(barware, glassware)

C'est Moi
3198 Paces Ferry Place
Atlanta, GA 30305
404/467-0095
(French glassware, ceramics, linens)

Crate & Barrel
800/451-8217 (for store locations)
800/323-5461 (for catalogue)
(barware, glassware, kitchenware)

Dean & Deluca
800/221-7714 (for catalogue)
www.dean-deluca.com
(caviar, gourmet foods, kitchenware)

DOM (USA), Inc.
693 Fifth Avenue
New York, NY 10012
212/334-5580
(glassware, kitchenware)

Fishs Eddy
889 Broadway
New York, NY 10003
212/420-9020
2176 Broadway
New York, NY 10024
212/873-8819
(retro china, glassware, housewares)

Felissimo
10 West 56th Street
New York, NY 10019
212/247-5656
(barware, glassware, kitchenware)

Galleri Orrefors Kosta Boda
58 East 57th Street
New, York, NY 10022
212/752-3705
(crystal stemware)

The Gourmet Food Store
847/244-9595 (for catalogue)
gourmetstore@sendit.com
(gourmet foods)

Hold Everything
800/421-2264 (for catalogue and store locations)
(glassware, housewares)

Home Depot
800/553-3199 (for store locations)
www.homedepot.com
(ceramic tiles, housewares)

Horchow Home
800/456-7000 (for catalogue)
(glassware, housewares)

IKEA
908/289-4488 (for West Coast store locations)
412/747-0747 (for East Coast store locations)
(glassware, housewares)

Lemon Grass
367 West Broadway
New York, NY 10013
212/343-0900
(candles)

Mood Indigo
181 Prince Street
New York, NY 10012
212/254-1176
(vintage barware, glassware)

Neiman Marcus
800/825-8000 (for catalogue and store locations)
(barware, glassware)

Pier 1 Imports, Inc.
800/245-4595 (for store locations)
www.pier1.com
(barware, glassware)

Pottery Barn
800/922-5507 (for catalogue)
800/-922-9934 (for store locations)
www.dreamshop.com
e-mail: dmg@tw.timeline.com
(barware, glassware, housewares)

Restoration Hardware
415/924-1005 (for store locations)
www.restorationhardware.com
(barware, housewares, linens)

Takashimaya, Inc.
693 Fifth Avenue
New York, New York 10012
212/350-0100
800/753-2038 (for catalogue)
(Japanese barware, housewares, linens)

Target Stores
612/304-6073 (call collect for store locations)
(glassware, kitchenware)

Tribeca Potters
443 Greenwich Street
New York, NY 10013
212/431-7631
(custom pottery)

Versace Fifth Avenue
647 Fifth Avenue, 5th floor
New York, NY 10022
212/317-0224
212/582-3473 (for additional store locations)
(barware, china, glassware)

Wolfman-Gold & Good Company
117 Mercer Street
New York, NY 10012
212/966-8268
(china, glassware, linens)

Williams-Sonoma
800/541-2233 (for catalogue)
800/541-1262 (for store locations)
www.dreamshop.com
(barware, glassware, kitchenware)

Zabar's
2245 Broadway
New York, NY 10024
212-787-2000
800-697-6301 (for catalogue)
(gourmet foods)

Zona
97 Greene Street
New York, NY 10012
212/925-6750
(glassware, housewares)

Whenever I look through these pages I will be reminded of Vivian Andres and the many hours we spent together designing this book. Her creativity and diligence far exceed her years, and I am proud to work so closely with this talented young designer. My husband, Doug, to whom this book is dedicated, has contributed his time, knowledge of mixology and unwavering support. My son Charley has been a welcome companion when burning the midnight oil. Thank you to my daughter Caroline, who grabs life with gusto and reminds me to embrace each day. I also want to thank my brother, John Faricy, for teaching me to celebrate with abandon the finer things in life. To Greg Sandberg and Vickie Ten Kate for their critical analysis during cocktail kitchen testing. Many kudos to chef Alix Kenagy for her wit, wisdom and remarkable culinary talent, and to photographer Jeff Von Hoene for his insistence on visual simplicity. Thanks to Matt De Galan and his uncanny ability to interpret my thoughts. I must thank my agent, Stedman Mays for laughing with me and believing in me. As always, I am grateful to my editor and friend, Suzanne De Galan, who is forever hip and usually right. And lastly, to my friends, to my relatives and to the readers of this book, with whom in some way I share the modern cocktail hour...to all of you - I raise my glass.

Add your name to the Modern mailing list! - call/fax - 770-594-0099